THE HISTORY AND SCIENCE BEHIND THE
WORLD'S BEST PIZZAS

By Jeffrey Merrihue

FRONT COVER PIZZAS:

Jeffrey Merrihue @ Pizzana, Los Angeles, CA

Fugazetta @ La Mezzetta, Buenos Aires, Argentina

"Jewish Pizza" @ Spago, Beverly Hills, CA

Deep Dish Pizza @ Pizzaria Uno, Chicago, IL

BACK COVER PIZZA:

Margherita Sbagliata @ Pepe in Grani, Caiazzo, Italy

Book design by Romney Lange

Printed and bound in the United States of America

First edition, printed 2019
ISBN: 978-1-54395-913-0

WELCOME TO THE WORLD'S FIRST MASTER CLASS IN PIZZA

Follow the chronological history of pizza from its traditional origins in 1738, delve into the science behind the making of superior pizza, hear from the leading *pizzaioli* and follow a map of where to eat the best examples of each regional pizza style around the world.

Read this book to visit these pizzerias in person or spirit, become a maestro in pizza and, most importantly, learn to enjoy pizza more — if that is even possible.

The author has lived in Italy and visited more than 2,000 around the world including each pizzeria referenced here. Along the way, he has interviewed numerous *pizzaioli* sweating away in front of their gorgeous ovens and added 10% to his body weight eating the world's favorite food.

SYNOPSIS

This book will track how ancient flatbreads blossomed into modern-day pizzas when tomatoes arrived in Naples in 1520. These original pizzas went on to beget dozens of regional styles around the world in three waves across seven global pizza centers: Naples, Buenos Aires, the New York pizza belt, Rome, Chicago, California and Old Forge, Pennsylvania.

Wave one lasted 170 years as Naples pizza makers invented and perfected the smaller original Neapolitan pizzas. Wave two lasted the next 100+ years as New Yorkers proved that necessity is the mother of invention leading to the bigger, crispier, drier, thicker and more complicated pizzas that evolved regionally across America. Wave three began in 2005 as the Italians reasserted their supremacy with a new wave of artisan pizzas.

The impact of the master *pizzaiolo* will be discussed as well.

The 7 Pizza Centers of the World

5th Pizza Center
CHICAGO

3rd Pizza Center
NEW YORK

4th Pizza Center
ROME

1st Pizza Center
NAPLES

7th Pizza Center
OLD FORGE, PA

6th Pizza Center
CALIFORNIA

2nd Pizza Center
BUENOS AIRES

THE HISTORY OF PIZZA

Flatbreads have existed for many centuries, with stories first emerging from Virgil referring to the idea of bread as an edible plate around 50 BC "See — we devour the plates on which we are fed." Stories from the Persian Empire in 500 BC told of the soldiers of King Darius the Great cooking flatbreads with cheese and dates on their shields over open fires. Arab lamechuns and Greek pitas date back over 1,000 years, while focaccia in Sicily and the *pinsas* from Rome also predate modern pizza by hundreds of years.

It wasn't until Spanish conquistador Hernan Cortes brought tomatoes to Italy from Latin America in 1520 that tomatoes made it onto flatbreads. The celebrated San Marzano tomatoes were first grown in volcanic soil in the shadow of Mount Vesuvius. One story goes that the first seed of this particular tomato came to Campania in 1770 as a gift from the Viceroyalty of Peru to the Kingdom of Naples. San Marzano's are the benchmark pizza tomato.

In the ensuing 200 years since the arrival of the tomato, flatbreads became a favorite food of the poor in Naples. Versions of pizza were sold from tin stoves balanced on the vendor's heads. Tomato pizzas were slow to evolve as many thought the nightshade to be poisonous. Samuel Morse — inventor of the telegraph — described pizza as "a most nauseating cake covered with slices of tomatoes and sprinkled with little fish (anchovies) and black pepper...it all together looks like a piece of bread that has been taken out of the sewer."

The History of Pizza

Alexandre Dumas, the author of *The Three Musketeers*, studied the poor of Naples, noting in 1835 that they existed exclusively on pizza in winter and watermelon in summer. He identified pizza as a barometer of the economy with marinara pizza prices rising when fish were scarce and falling when fish were plentiful. A structure of pizza pricing existed with fresh pizza costing more than day-old pizza and stale pizza available for even less. There was a pizza credit system called Pizza al Otto, meaning you could pay for your stale pizza 8 days later, which then became known as "the last supper" if you died in the interim. This piece of history is a dramatic reminder of how pizza rose from the food of the poor to become the world's favorite food.

The world's first pizzeria, **Antica Pizzeria Port'alba** (1738) was established in Naples as a stand for the tin stove vendors. A world treasure, with its oven lined with lava rocks from Mount Vesuvius, it is still in operation today in the town center. In 1889, Raffaele Esposito from **Pizzeria Brandi** (1870) in Naples created pizzas for the visiting King Umberto and Queen Margherita de Savoy. Her favorite pie featured the colors of the Italian flag with red (tomato), white (cheese) and green (basil). The queen loved the combination, leading to the pizza being named after her. A letter of gratitude hangs at Brandi today.

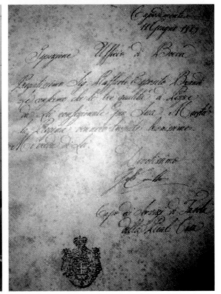

The History of Pizza

Since then, the Neapolitan Margherita pizza has become known the world over for its characteristics: smaller 10-inch discs with little more than tomato, cheese and basil presented in a wet style that benefits from a knife and fork.

Naples' forefathers created a society — the AVPN — Associazione Verace de Pizza Napolitano to protect and promote these characteristics and the city of Naples was rewarded for these 300 years of effort with a UNESCO designation of the cultural heritage of humanity in 2017. The spread of its craft has ensured a great Neapolitan pizza is available in most major cities around the world.

Pizza Marinara is the less famous cousin and is essentially a cheeseless Margherita that was named after sailors who appreciated the ingredients that were easy to store and transport.

# The History of Pizza

The next historical wave started when Genaro Lombardi opened the 1st American pizzeria in New York City in 1905. As Italian immigration swelled, a pizza belt was established from Philadelphia to New Haven and up to Boston. Rome and Chicago followed, to lay claim to pizza royalty status only since World War II. Some traditionalists argue that Neapolitans are the only true pizzas and that all other pizza styles are derivative and secondary. The resulting arguments can reach the same "shouting match" levels as other life-and-death debates, like whether tacos should be soft or crunchy, or whether or not you should put ketchup on a hot dog. Neapolitans are great, but so are the wave of regional pizzas that flourished in New York, Rome, Chicago and beyond.

These regional pizzas are every bit as good as the Neapolitans but they are very different. These styles have become bigger, thicker, drier, chewier and crunchier than Neapolitans. Indeed, some innovators are achieving exciting contrasts such as crunchier and softer in the same pizza like our entry from Copenhagen.

Today there is also a new generation of classically trained chefs and bakers who are experimenting with new approaches to baking the crust as well as innovative toppings and even formats (pizza cones). The remaining history will be expressed in the following stories about the 7 pizza centers and their representative pizzerias.

THE SCIENCE OF PIZZA

Our approach here will be to establish the technical specifications of the Neapolitan pizza and then to identify how its pizza descendants differ. Here are the eight ingredients of the Margherita pizza: water, flour, salt, yeast, tomatoes, cheese, basil and olive oil. The ensuing variations are infinite.

Flour - Almost all Naples pizzerias use a powdery wonder called "00" from a single family mill in Naples called Molino Caputo (1924). They mill several kinds of wheat 25 times to achieve the fine texture ideal for pizza and sell a blue bag version with 12.5% gluten for the Neapolitan pizzas and a 13.5% version for "sturdier" American style pizzas. In the US, gluten (protein) levels go up to 14%.

Water - Not much to say about water except that lower minerality waters are best for Neapolitan pizzas and "harder" waters are better for the more robust American pizzas. Obviously chlorinated and other intrusive water should be avoided.

Yeast - Ancient Egyptians discovered yeast accidentally when leaving water and flour in the sun causing a natural fermentation that would have produced better bread. Yeast converts sugars into alcohol, which is why beer and pizza go so well together. It also releases bubbles that cause the dough to rise and become both light and chewy simultaneously. This effect is why well-made pizza is not as filling as one might expect. Neapolitans require fresh yeast that stores for 2 weeks, while most American pizzerias use active dry yeast (stores for 2 months). No decent pizzas use quick-rise or frozen yeast.

Starters - Although starters are not permitted by APVN, they are being adopted to trigger the fermentation process as they often impart a "fresh bread" flavor, an "airier" texture and easier-to-digest dough. Starters are often saved from batch to batch with some known to have been passed down from generation to generation. Many bakers swear by starters.

The Science of Pizza

Dough – Water, salt, flour and yeast are the only ingredients of Neapolitan pizza dough. Olive oil is added to achieve the crispy and fried qualities of Roman, Sicilian, Grandma and Detroit style pizzas. The Neapolitan doughs rise for 2 hours and then 6 more hours. Many fancier pizzas use dough that rises for up to 60 hours. Short proof times lead to the softer, chewier pizzas like the Neapolitans, while longer proof times yield more durable thicker crusts. The Neapolitans are uniquely smaller at 10" as if they were any bigger the crust would fall apart. The dough may be machine mixed for AVPN but can only be hand rolled. Not even rolling pins are allowed. Roman and New York pizzas with higher gluten levels, lower humidity levels and longer proof times yield the more robust and crispier pizza styles.

Fuel - There is a romantic hierarchy that descends from wood-fired Neapolitan pizzas to coal-fired New York and New Haven pizzas and to (supposedly) inferior gas-fired and electric oven pizzas. In general, that hierarchy has some merit as wood imparts a smokiness that is unique. But this advantage is challenged when you try excellent gas-fired pizzas from places like Di Fara (1959) in Brooklyn and superb coal-fired pizzas from places like Frank Pepe's (1925) whose New Haven website complains that wood gives off steam while coal burns hot and dry! Jon and Vinny's in Los Angeles also produces an excellent electric oven pizza.

Baking - Neapolitan pizzas are baked from 60 to 90 seconds at between 800 and 900 degrees while New York and other bigger and thicker pizzas bake anywhere from 2–5 minutes at between 500–700 degrees. For really hot temperatures brick- and stone-lined ovens are required. In Naples, many use volcanic rock from Vesuvius, which adds both better temperature diffusion and maintenance as well as a dash of romance. In the oven the Neapolitans are turned once and pulled out. Other pies may be turned multiple times and some are lifted to catch a dose of wood flame for smokiness and extra blistering.

Tomatoes – The benchmark tomatoes are the pear-shaped, canned San Marzano tomatoes grown around the base of Mount Vesuvius. They are perfect for pizza due to their sweet taste, low acidity and high consistency. The surprising fresh taste of these canned tomatoes is because they are "picked and packed" the same day in a highly manual harvesting and canning process. Pizza novices are often surprised that fresh tomatoes do not play a major role in most pizzas (although both fresh and canned are permitted by AVPN). The fact is tomatoes are notoriously variable in texture and quality from season to season and the canned San Marzano tomatoes provide the consistency needed to create a great pizza. Another way to think of it is that in a process that suffers from excess variability, canned San Marzanos are a source of reliability. Note that pizza sauces are very different from the thick, rich pasta sauces that benefit from simmering overnight. However, 95% of cans sold are fake, so look for the double DOP seals and certificate number on the bottom or sides of the cans. The fakes are materially inferior.

The Science of Pizza

Cheese – Mozzarella is a name derived from the Italian word to pinch when cutting the cheese. Mozzarella is made with cow milk (Fior de Latte) which is smooth, silky and milky, is brined and cut into strips. Buffalo mozzarella (mozzarella di bufala) is more full flavored and robust but releases more moisture that can make already wet Neapolitan pizzas even soggier. Most pizza fanatics prefer buffalo but only in the hands of very skilled *pizzaiolo*. In the USA the go-to mozzarella is known as a "Caprese Loaf" which is a low-moisture dry mozzarella that is vacuum packed and is often hand grated onto the sturdier pizzas. Burrata is a mozzarella filled with cream and curds sometimes used as a super creamy specialty ingredient added to pizza after baking.

A key difference in fresh-brined mozzarella on a Neapolitan style pizza is it must be eaten straight out of the oven, while the drier New York pies are great for delivery and even taste good the next morning.

Both Neapolitans and New Yorks often benefit from a sprinkle of parmigiano-reggiano, grana padano or pecorino on top.

Toppings – AVPN requires extra-virgin olive oil and encourages garlic and oregano. New Yorkers contributed pepperoni to the topping world, which is on 36% of American pizzas. California then triggered the onslaught of all kinds of farm-to-pizza toppings. The most notorious contribution was from a Greek immigrant in Toronto who invented the Hawaiian pizza at the Satellite (1962) restaurant. This pizza is based on the Chinese sweet-and-sour pork dish with pineapple and ham and is generally hated by pizza purists.

THE PROBLEM WITH PIZZA

The rules for Neapolitan pizza are very clear and many regional innovations seem straightforward on paper, so why is great pizza so hard to make? The reason is that dough is affected by small changes in environment. For example, as a pizzeria heats up during the day, changes in temperature and moisture can cause the dough to harden or fall apart. The levels of wood or coal and the numbers of pizzas being made at any given time can change the outcome significantly. The moisture levels in the cheese and/or tomatoes can vary even from cheese to cheese and tomato to tomato.

These ever-changing micro-conditions can overwhelm the quality of ingredients and wreak havoc on great pizza recipes. A baker faces many of these challenges, but when resolved, she bakes all of her bread at the same time. Pizzas get made one by one in conditions that change hourly. This is where a skilled, individual *pizzaiolo* can evaluate a dough and make adjustments to compensate for the infinite number of hurdles that bedevil the process.

The best can deliver exceptional pizza consistently under highly variable conditions. This also explains why your favorite pizza may not be great the next time out. It also explains why old-time pizzerias with long-serving employees remain great for years and decades as they retain skills that are not present in newer pizzerias.

1ST CENTER: NAPLES

The Birthplace of Pizza

The history of Naples is covered previously, so here we will shine a light on three of the most influential pizzerias. Although it should be noted that 15 to 20 more could easily be covered in a more comprehensive review of influential pizzerias.

Antica Pizzeria Port'Alba – The World's 1st Pizzeria

Antica Pizzeria Port'Alba (1738), was established in Naples as a stand for street vendors who kept pizzas hot in small tin stoves balanced on their heads. It then converted into the world's 1st pizzeria in 1830. A world treasure, with its oven lined with lava rocks from Mount Vesuvius, it is still in operation today in the town center and the pizzas on the simple menu are traditional and lovely. A visit here is your 1st essential step toward a true understanding of the history of pizza.

La Antica Pizzeria Brandi – The Margherita Pizza Is Born

In 1889, Queen Margherita of Savoy was in Naples to celebrate the reclamation of the city. She wanted to try the city's most famous dish and summoned the head *pizzaiolo* — Raffaele Esposito from Pizzeria Brandi (1780). He served traditional pizzas from Naples including the classic with cheese, tomato and basil, which the queen loved as apart from being delicious it featured the colors of the Italian flag: tomato (red), cheese (white) and basil (green). She then sent a letter of appreciation that can still be seen at the pizzeria and which caused the pizza to be dubbed the "Margherita" and history was made.

Antica Pizzeria Port'Alba – Pizza Marinara. Image courtesy of gennaro_luciano_maestro.

Pizzeria Brandi - Pizza Margherita. Image courtesy of eatammece.

L'Antica Pizzeria Da Michele

Da Michele (1906) was immortalized in 2010 by Julia Roberts in *Eat, Pray, Love*. Beyond the hype, the pizza is great. If you can score the table next to the oven, you can experience the pizza being made, baked in the oven and served piping hot right in front of you in under 90 seconds. They spin the dough ball flat in three spins, spread it straight on the pizza peel and bake it for 60 seconds before popping it hot on to your table. The quality and an intangible magic enshrine Michele as the finest combination of taste, experience and tradition for Neapolitan pizza.

L'Antica Pizzeria da Michele - Pizza Margherita. Image courtesy of L'Antica Pizzeria Da Michele.

2ND CENTER: BUENOS AIRES

The First Quiet Wave

Most pizza lovers think pizza went straight from Naples to New York and are unaware of the pizza capital of Latin America that predated the New York revolution. In Buenos Aires you will find supremely high quality pizza with a distinct personality, as well as the mighty fugazetta which should be enshrined as an UNESCO treasure. While the southern Italians went to New York, the northerners went to Buenos Aires. It is therefore not surprising that New York style pizza is a thinner, tomato-based pizza while in Buenos Aires you find thicker, cheese-based pizzas. The 1st recorded pizza was 7 years before the invention of the Margherita in Naples by a Neapolitan baker Nicolas Vaccarezza who sold a simple recipe of dough, garlic, olive oil and onion from a rented oven on the streets in "La Boca" neighborhood in 1882.

Augustin Banchero then created the legendary cheesy "Fugazetta" in his bakery Riachuelo (1889). His son Juan then founded Banchero (1932). His contribution of Fugazetta to Pizzadom is truly epic. It is a deep dish of onions, mozzarella, black pepper and olive oil. Las Cuartetas (1936) is also famous locally for the Pizza Salvatore made with mozzarella and anchovies. Since then Las Cuarteta and other famous pizzerias like El Guerrin (1932) and El Cuartito (1934) have served these regional specialties to an adoring Buenos Aires. The best Fugazetta is served at La Mezzetta (1939) — make sure to order it with the edible chickpea plates that slide under or on top of the slice and which you will see nowhere else.

La Mezzetta – Fugazetta. Image courtesy of panzallena.ba.

3RD CENTER: NEW YORK

The "Pizza Belt" Is Established

New York pizzerias often bill themselves as Neapolitan because that is where their founders were born but that designation or even Neapolitan-American is misleading. These two pizza styles are different in every way. Neapolitan pizzas are wood-fired while the wide availability of coal in the USA in the early 1900s meant the pizza pioneers of New York used coal. The Neapolitans make a smaller, wetter, simpler and in many ways more elegant pizza while the New Yorkers are bigger, more charred and feature many more toppings, including pepperoni, which was an entirely American creation by the butchers around Bleeker Street 1st cited in 1919.

Here are some highlights of the many differences in pizza styles:

PIZZA STYLE	NEAPOLITAN	NEW YORK
Size	10"	18"
Dough	Hand kneaded	Hand tossed
Dough	Moist 70% +	Drier 60% +
Flour	Fine, powdery – lower gluten	Coarser – higher gluten
Cheese	Fresh-cut mozzerella	Dry-grated mozzerella
Sauce	Ladled on uncooked	Simmered previously
Water	Soft medium	Mineral rich
Outcome	Smaller, softer and wetter	Bigger, chewer and drier
Char	Light	Darker char

The original **Lombardi's** (1905) sprouted a vast and contentious family tree of New York pizzerias that firmly established New York as a distinct style of pizza. This distinction in pizza style is crucial as the birth of New York pizza kicked off the 2nd 100 years of innovation in regional pizza styles as the Americans took the lead in pizza innovation.

Lombardi's was where the *pizzaioli* worked from an astounding array of the greatest New York pizzerias. The students of Lombardi's went on to Totonno's (1924) in Coney Island, John's of Bleeker St (1929), Patsy's (1933) in East Harlem and Grimaldi's (1941) in Brooklyn. Patsy Grimaldi owns a special place in history having opened an outpost called Patsy's (then losing the name), renaming it Grimaldi's (which he sold), and then, when the original Grimaldi's moved a few doors down, opening again in the original spot as Juliana's (2012), named after his mother. A pro tip is to try Juliana's and Grimaldi's back to back as they are next to each other, and decide for yourself which of the feuding pizzerias makes the best pizza. Our pick is the original Patsy's in East Harlem where they reportedly invented the slice of New York pizza and where the pepperoni still tastes best.

Patsy's Pizzeria. Image courtesy of wikipedia.

John's of Bleeker Street. Image courtesy of wikipedia.

New York and the Pizza Belt

Lombardi's

Gennaro Lombardi started the business in 1897 as a grocery store at 53½ Spring Street and began selling tomato pies wrapped in paper and tied with a string at lunchtime to workers from the area's factories. In 1905 Lombardi received a license to operate a pizzeria, and soon had a loyal clientele, including Italian tenor Enrico Caruso. Lombardi's is where the major New York pizza dynasties got their start, including Totonno's, John's, Patsy's and Grimaldi's. This is an essential pizzeria for historical reasons but the pizza is outstanding on its own merits.

Di Fara

If there is any question about the potential excellence of gas-fired ovens try one of the most lauded pizzas in the world at Di Fara (1959). Each pizza is made by Dom DiMarco who makes each pie from fresh dough. His recipe is unique using a mix of canned San Marzano tomatoes and fresh tomatoes as well as ¾ buffalo mozzarella and ¼ American mozzarella "Grande" with a sprinkle of grana padano at the end. With oregano imported from Israel and fresh basil on his windowsill, Dom is one of the great *pizzaiolo* legends.

Di Fara Pizza. Image courtesy of noahfecksisawesome.

Lombardi's – Pepperoni Pizza. Image courtesy of zzachhonig.

Other Influential Pizzas in the Pizza Belt

Make sure to stop on Staten Island for great pizza at Denino's (1937), Lee's Tavern (1940) and Joe & Pats (1960) before arriving in New Jersey to try Papa's (1912). Papa's is the longest continuously open pizzeria in America because Lombardi's closed for several years during the 80s. Papa's is also known for its inverted "Tomato Pies" that lay down the cheese (very little) first and then the tomatoes. A related phenomenon can be found in Philadelphia where bakeries serve rectangular trays of tomato pies with no cheese at all. They are baked in the morning and served fresh with Iannelli's Bakery (1910) laying claim to one of the oldest and best.

The best *pizzaiolo* you have never heard of is Dan Richer, the owner of Razza Pizza Artiginale (2013) from Jersey City. His pursuit of bread and butter perfection results in pizza that is simply outstanding. His wood-fired pies feature a local buffalo mozzarella and tomatoes sourced from the USA and Italy that are blended for optimum results. There is real artisan talent on display in these pizzas and don't forget to try the stunning bread and butter while you are there.

Dan Richer. Image courtesy of Razza Pizza Artiginale.

Razza Pizza Artiginale. Image courtesy of Razza Pizza Artiginale.

Other Influential Pizzas in the Pizza Belt

Heading north to New Haven you will find the home of Apizza. *A-Beetz* is a local Italian-American dialect that took hold in this pizza-mad city. Here you will find the world-renowned pioneer **Frank Pepe** (1925) who is known for his tomato pies as well as for inventing the fresh clam white pie in 1950. Pepe boasts about their coal-fired brick oven burning hot and dry compared to wood-fired ovens that "give off steam"! In a further historical contribution, they were credited with using women's corset boxes as the world's 1st pizza boxes. Nearby **Modern** (1934) placed the 1st known order for actual pizza boxes in 1945. Among a dozen other renowned pizzerias, a hidden gem can be found over in West Haven where **Zuppardi's** (1932) bakes a fresh clam pie to rival Frank Pepe. History buffs will find all kinds of other tidbits (supplied by New Haven historian Colin Caplan) including New Haven origins for the 1st American pizza truck, vending machine, home pizza kit and advertisement to students at Yale.

Farther up the road in Boston is **Santarpio's** (1933) which does a sausage and garlic pie that is truly remarkable as well as a bakery — **Parziales** (1907) — that challenges Papa's as the longest "continuously running" pizzeria in the USA. All of these pizzerias are at the heart of major Italian-American immigrant populations stretching from Philadelphia to Boston.

Zuppardi's – Fresh Clam Pizza. Image courtesy of Zuppardi's Apizza.

Santarpio's – Sausage and Garlic Pizza. Image courtesy of Jeffrey Merrihue.

Frank Pepe – Tomato Pizza. Image courtesy of Frank Pepe.

Frank Pepe – White Clam Pizza. Image courtesy of Frank Pepe.

4TH CENTER: ROME

A Sleeping Giant Awakens

Rome can be credited with creating the flatbreads known as *pinsas* in 200 AD that became the base of modern pizza. Although showing early promise, Rome somehow missed out on the first 170-year frenzy of modern pizza making despite being only 3 hours north of Naples. However, when Rome finally got with the program, they contributed two massive regional styles to the world:

La Pratolina – Pinsa. Image courtesy of mascamenny.

crispy thin crust and thick, yeasty *Pizza al taglio*. Try the *pinsas* at the excellent La Pratolina (2001) by the Coliseum.

The restaurant Est, Est Est (1888) became Rome's 1st pizzeria in the early 1900s when the pizza oven was added. It was decades later before pizza took off but the Romans caught on quickly with the thin crispy crust pizzas that are a vivid contrast to the soft, wet Neapolitans down the road.

The Romans add olive oil to the dough (an AVPN crime), flatten the edges and cook at lower temperatures (around 500 degrees) with longer bake times of 2–3 minutes to get a thinner *cornicione* and a crispier, cracker-like center. This is a very significant difference between two of the world's great pizza centers. Two great spots for these classic pizzas are **Da Remo** (1976) and the beloved **Li Rioni** (1986).

Rome also contributed a focaccia-like *pizza al taglio* which are cut with scissors by the slice and sold by weight. Rome also birthed two pizza geniuses: Stefano Callegari discussed in this section and Gabrielle Bionci discussed later in the Future of Pizza.

Pizza al Taglio.

Li Rioni – Margherita Pizza. Image courtesy of everythingfrank.

4th Center – Rome

Sforno

Stefano Callegari burst upon the pizza world with a truly excellent pizzeria featuring classic Roman pizzas as well as inventing the infamous Cacio y Pepe pizza with a pepper grinder smack in the middle.

Most inventors would have been fine with that but he and his partners went on to open Trapizzino (formerly 00100) where they invented the pizza sandwich, which is essentially a focaccia stuffed with Roman delicacies like oxtail. Stefano is at the intersection of tradition and innovation and is a worthy candidate for the pizza "hall of fame" especially since he loves ultra-charred crusts (as do I).

Trapizzino.

Stefano Callegari. Image courtesy Trapizzino.

Sforno – Cacio e Peppe Pizza. Image courtesy of flaminia_ds.

 # 5TH CENTER: CHICAGO

The Deep Dish Phenomenon

Gas-fired deep dish has put Chicago into the big leagues with Naples, New York and Rome. It all began at Pizzeria Uno (1943) that then spawned a family tree of great Chicago pizzas. From Uno followed Pizzeria Due, and then Gino's East (1966) took off when two taxi drivers snatched Alice, the *Pizzaiola* from Uno to copy and spread deep dish fever. Rudy Sr.'s son Lou launched Lou Malnatti's (1971) which some aficionados believe to be the tastiest chain with an entire wall-to-wall sausage layer placed over the cheese (and under the tomatoes). When he first opened on St. Patrick's Day, he famously quipped: He opened an Italian restaurant in a Jewish neighborhood on an Irish holiday. Finally, Rudy Malnatti Jr. launched Pizano (1991) to keep the family tradition alive. Both of the Malnatti brothers pizzas feature "butter crusts" instead of olive oil and have less toppings than their imitators, offering a "slightly lighter" experience. While New York is a pepperoni town, Chicago is firmly sausage. The standout deep dish pizza in Chicago is the carmelized "burnt crust" beauty from Pequods (1970).

Pizzaria Uno

Deep dish started in Chicago at the corner of Ohio & Wabash. Ike Sewell, an ex-University of Texas football star decided to open a restaurant with his pal Ric Riccardo. Bemoaning wimpy Italian pizzas they recruited Rudy Malnatti and Alice May Redmond to come up with a "more substantial" pizza. The recipe is ingenious with the dough being pressed into a deep olive oily pan that fires the crust crispy. The 2nd innovation was to invert the layers with the cheese going on 1st so it would not burn. The cheese is then followed by the "toppings" in the middle with the crushed tomatoes going on last. Historic!

Pizzeria Uno. Image courtesy of mariasilviaat.

6TH CENTER: CALIFORNIA

Farm to Table Lands on Pizza

Pizzas topped with farmers market ingredients were invented by Jeremiah Tower in 1974 at Chez Panisse. When he ran out of standard pizza ingredients, they covered the pie in seafood left over from the bouillabaisse the night before. Alice Waters went on to perfect a nettle pizza for which she became famous and which is still often on the menu. The California pizza boom really took off in 1980 when Wolfgang Puck was blown away by a mustard, ricotta, pate and red pepper pizza served by Ed LeDou who was experimenting at a restaurant called Prego in San Francisco. Wolfgang hired Ed to make pizzas at Spago where he became notorious for a "Jewish Pizza" made with salmon, crème fraiche — and later caviar — which became a signature dish at the restaurant and Oscar parties.

Ed later went on to consult for California Pizza Kitchen where he invented the BBQ chicken pizza that put California pizza on the national map. This approach made it back to London when Jason Atherton at Maze grated white truffles onto a crispy flatbread with onion puree, white truffle paste, fontina cheese, mozzarella, pancetta, ceps and fresh herbs for over $100 a pop.

San Francisco has a prominent baking community and pizza tradition that dates back to Tomasso's (1935). The Cantalupo family who had immigrated from Italy installed the West Coast's 1st wood-burning brick oven. Both Alice Waters and Wolfgang Puck are said to have modeled their pizza initiatives after Tomasso's.

Spago's "Jewish Pizza." Image courtesy of Jeffrey Merrihue.

6th Center – California

Another innovator is Cheeseboard Collective (1991) who have been baking for 50 years. They started in the late 80s smearing their cheeses on hot sourdough for their co-workers and originated the one-pizza-a-day offering with vegetarian pies made with all kinds of cheese (no tomato sauce).

While speaking of cheese I would like to make this books only reference to focaccia. La Manuelina located in Recco just south of Genoa is credited with inventing "cheesy focaccia" and it is a wonder to behold. Nancy Silverton from Mozza LA was so taken with this that when she returned from Recco she and her team made over 200 trials to replicate it. Would it be sacrilege to say that the one she conjured up at Chi Spacca is even better than the original?

A special shout goes to Tony Gemignani. He first became known for his pizza tossing acrobatics but then went on to astonish the pizza world by winning the World Pizza Championship in Naples, Italy, in 2007— he was the first non-Italian to achieve this feat. He also invented a unique four-oven (Cuatro Forni) pizza at his restaurant Capo (2012) in San Francisco. In some ways, Tony crowned 100 years of American pizza achievement in 2007 by snatching the crown from the Italians at the same time that a revolution was unfolding back in Italy as the third wave of pizza innovation took off.

Tony Gemignani, San Francisco. Image courtesy of wikipedia.

Chez Panisse – Pizza topped with egg. Image courtesy of wikipedia.

Cheeseboard Collective – Berkeley Pizza. Image courtesy of Christina Diaz.

7TH CENTER: OLD FORGE

The World's Most Fanatical Pizza Town

It is only fitting that our last pizza center be a tiny pizza-crazed town that no one has heard of. A Northeast Pennsylvania town that has proclaimed itself the "Pizza Capital of the World," Old Forge is a former coal-mining town of about 8,000 which is 45% Italian with most of the residents being descendants of a single town by the name of Felitto, near Naples. There are a dozen pizzerias in this tiny town. Old Forge–style pizza was created by Nonna Ghigiarelli, who made it for regulars of her family bar back in 1926. While Elio G's (G for Ghigiarelli) is thriving, the original location next door called Ghigiarelli where the pizza was invented is shuttered due to a Hollywood-style murder mystery where the owner mysteriously disappeared leaving a blood-splattered trail from his restaurant to an abandoned car.

Returning to the pizza, you find a unique language where pies are called trays — cooked in square pans — and slices are called cuts. The cheeses are a blend including mozzarella, cheddar, provolone and even American cheese. The sauce often has a heavy onion profile. The red pizzas are a deep-pan style with the sauce on top while the whites are like a Chicago stuffed pizza. It seems only right to finish our review of pizza centers with the most pizza-crazy town in the world.

Elio G's – Old Forge Red and White Pizza. Image courtesy of sara_cornelius.

ARTISAN PIZZA IN ITALY

Artisan Pizza Being Reinvented Back in Italy

Gabriele Bonci was a chef who started the third wave artisan pizza revolution in Rome with the opening of **Pizzarium** in 2003. He overhauled the traditional process of pizza making by keeping the best parts and improving steps that had become less relevant. He started with sourdough starter dating back to World War I and proofed the dough for up to 72 hours with the addition of olive oil to produce rectangular trays of thick, bubble-ridden crusts that were deceptively light. Featuring 20 varying toppings a day from traditional rosso to flowers to cured rabbit, adding up to 1,500 varieties per year.

Pizzaium pizza. Image courtesy of Pizzarium.

Franco Pepe furthered the revolution when he opened **Pepe in Grani** (2012) between Rome and Naples. He was a baker first who revised each process step. Franco pioneered so-called "zero kilometer" sourcing by ensuring that each ingredient came from within 5 kilometers of his pizzeria. Today, he has continued to innovate with a tasting menu that includes the *Ciro*: a pizza cone filled with grana padano cream and pesto. Boom!

Pepe in Grani, "Ciro". Image courtesy of Jeffrey Merrihue.

Artisan Pizza in Italy

Renato Bosco completes the Italian trio of **Pizza Da Vincis** in the unlikely city of Verona. He too comes from a baker background and has reinvented dough at his pizzeria Sapore (2009). His pizzas go from yeast-less flat pies to ultra fluffy focaccias. He has trademarked his specialty pie which he calls "Doppio Crunch" — essentially a focaccia stuffed with pizza. His tagline? "Do not wait for the same old pizza."

A further tip of the hat must go to Enzo Coccia at La Notizia in Naples for his dedication to teaching and educating about pizza skills. I **Tigli** in Verona came out 1st in a Gambero Rosso list of best Italian pizzas in 2012. His $40 creations are straight from the California Pizza Kitchen school. This honor was clouded, however, by the list not featuring a single Naples pizzeria that year!

Renato Bosco's "Doppio Crunch". Image courtesy of www.scattidigusto.it.

A FEW COMMENTS ABOUT OTHER PROMINENT PIZZA CENTERS

ITALY: One might think there are 1000s of great pizzerias in Italy but because pizzas are very inexpensive they do not motivate chefs to buy the best ingredients. I lived in Italy and tried hundreds of pizzas and agree with the conclusions of **Lorenzo Franceschi-Bicchierai** who concluded that most pizzas in New York are better than most pizzas in Italy.

BRAZIL: This country has the highest per capita consumption of pizza in the world and indeed on Sundays, families dress up in their finery and go for pizza. The pizzas, in general, lack character and regional flair even at the most celebrated spots, like **Braz In Sao Paolo**.

JAPAN: Pizza in Tokyo has come a long way, and many folks trumpet Japanese pizzas from **Seirinkan**, **Pizza Studio Tamaki** and **Savoy** as world class. Indeed, they have made great strides with their AVPN-compliant Margheritas and Marinaras as they have achieved lovely charred and blistered crusts but their sauces are often under-seasoned and watery and, as a result, the pizzas are not as harmonious as they should be. I suspect they will continue to improve in the future because the Japanese are perfectionists!

Pizza Studio Tamaki. Image courtesy of The Japan Times.

OTHER GREAT PIZZAS AROUND THE WORLD

There are some great deep dish pizzas around the world, starting with a legend on the far west coast of Sicily. Calvino (1946) is the definitive classic thick crust and trademark oblong shape. Uniquely, there is no sauce — just cherry tomatoes!

The benchmark Sicilian pizza in New York is L&B Spumoni Gardens (1939) which is a neighborhood gem that makes the best Sicilian pizzas outside of Sicily. In Detroit, Buddy's speakeasy (1936) began making rectangular tray pizza in 1946 that has recently become popular across America at great places like at Emmy Squared in Brooklyn. A similar style called Grandma was created on Long Island when King Umberto's (1976) started selling pizzas to customers that employees had been making for themselves.

Two other American pizzerias deserve mention. Pizzeria Bianco (1987) became an urban legend in the totally NOT pizza center of Phoenix in 1987 when Chris Bianco began making every pizza by hand with house-made mozzarella and grew his own basil. He now mostly supervises what still remain excellent pizzas at his various locations. Al Forno (1980) in New Jersey serves a truly innovative pizza created by mistake when they ended up grilling a pizza over coal flipping it and adding the toppings – an oddball classic.

L&B Spumoni Gardens – Sicilian Pizza. Image Courtesy of Jeffrey Merrihue.

Other Great Pizzas Around the World

In a quiet corner of middle England Story Deli (2010) makes the world's most innovative pizza. Artist Ann Shore and her husband, Lee Hollingworth make an organic, yeast-free-cracker thin crust that makes thin Roman pizza seem like deep dish. Up in Copenhagen, fans talk about Baest (2014) that featured in Ugly – Delicious but really the action is over at Neighbourhood (2015) where they acknowledge and pay homage to Story Deli with a similar cracker thin beauty that has a softer center for contrast.

So with writer's prerogative, I would like to finish this treatise with a nod to my favorite pizza I have tried this year — I Masanielli in Caserta (near Naples) where the famous buffalo mozzarella comes from. Francisco Martucci (and his younger brother Sasa in a nearby shop) make the world's most exciting pizzas in the shadow of pizza giant Franco Pepe, which gets most of the press and glory. I am a huge fan of Franco, and admire the way he continues to innovate but Martucci has focused all of his energy on making the perfect pizza with it's amazing "crunch" crust.

I Masanielli Pizzeria Da Francesco Martucci. Image courtesy of eat_food_prn.

Story Deli – Margherita Pizza. Image Courtesy of Gareth Agius.

SUMMARY

As described above, there have been 280 years of pizza history so far. The 1st 170 year wave of pizza innovation was dominated by Italy. The 2nd 100-year wave of regional pizza innovation was dominated by the Americans. This 2nd wave peaked in 2007 when Tony Gemignani became the first American (and indeed, non-Italian) to win the World Pizza Championships in Naples.

In the past 15 years, the 3rd wave of artisan innovation has swung firmly back to Italy with Bonci, Bosco, Martucci and Pepe leading the way.

It will be interesting to see what the Japanese do and to watch (and eat) where pizza, the world's favorite food, goes in the coming decades.

The research here reflects a debt of gratitude to the XtremeFoodies experts in each city and to my good friend Daniel Young, whose landmark book *Where to Eat Pizza* should be owned by all serious pizza lovers.

MEET THE AUTHOR

Jeffrey Merrihue

Jeffrey Merrihue is the founder of XtremeFoodies and Mofilm. Mofilm provides short-form videos to big brands like Coca-Cola, Visa and PlayStation as well as The World's 50 Best Restaurants.

He has eaten at all 135 restaurants that have been on the World's 50 Best lists since 2005. After 30 years living in Europe and Latin America, his wife and three kids have moved to Los Angeles to enjoy the weather, the epic Chinese and Korean food and...oh...those tacos!

Also look for Jeffrey who is a judge on Iron Chef Canada.

Follow him on Instagram @jeffrey_merrihue

XTREME FOODIES

XtremeFoodies searches for, discovers, celebrates and shares the world's most Essential Eats. As the world's largest network of local food experts from over 275 cities, we are on a mission to find the tastiest locally sourced and freshly prepared food from all around the globe.

Our local food experts are prominent food specialists, who use years of local expertise to handpick the Essential Eats in their region, giving you an insight into food that is not only delicious, but that also reflects the authentic cultures, traditions and trends of their local neighborhoods, cities and regions.

To find the Essential Eats near you on the go, we not only have our mobile-friendly site, but we have also developed an app that allows you to easily track the best places to eat wherever you travel.

Visit: www.xtremefoodies.com
You can also find us on Facebook, Instagram and Twitter.

Pictured on the right: Jeffrey Merrihue with Master Pizzaioli:
Daniel Uditi @Pizzana, Los Angeles, CA (top left)
Enzo Coccia @Notizia, Naples, Italy (top right)
Francesco Martucci @I Masanelli, Caserta, Italy (left)
Franco Pepe @Pepe in Grani, Naples, Italy (right)

PIZZARIAS

AlForno
484 US Highway 202, Flemington, NJ 08822
USA

Antica Pizzeria Port'alba
Gennaro Luciano
Via Port'Alba, 18, 80134 Napoli NA,
Italy

Baest
Chef Christian Puglisi
Guldbergsgade 29, 2200 København,
Denmark

Banchero
Juan Banchero
Av. Corrientes 1300, C1043AAZ CABA,
Argentina

Braz Pizzaria
Rua Sergipe, 406 - Consolação
São Paulo - SP 01243-000, Brazil

Buddy's
Robert Jacobs
19163, Mack Avenue, Grosse Pointe, MI 48236,
USA

Calvino
Via Nunzio
Nasi, 71, 91100 Trapani TP, Italy

Capo
Tony Gemignani
641 Vallejo St, San Francisco, CA 94133, USA

Da Remo
Piazza di Santa Maria Liberatrice, 44 00153
Rome, Italy

Denino's
Carlo Denino
524 Port Richmond Ave., Staten Island, NY 10302
USA

Di Fara
Domenico De Marco
1424 Avenue J Brooklyn, NY 11230, USA

El Cuartito
Talcahuano 937, Buenos Aires, Capital Federal
Argentina

El Guerrin
Mr. Guido Grondona and Franco Malvezzi
Av. Corrientes 1368, C1043ABN Buenos Aires,
Autónoma de Buenos Aires, Argentina

Elio G's Pizza
843 S Main St, Old Forge, PA 18518,
USA

Emmy Squared
Matt Hyland
364 Grand Street,
Brooklyn, NY 11211 USA

Frank Pepe
Frank Pepe
163 Wooster Street, New Haven, CT 06511, USA

Gino's East
Sam Levine, Fred Bartoli and George Loverde
162 E Superior Street (8,540.47 mi)
Chicago, IL 60654, USA

I Masanielli Pizzeria Da Francesco Martucci
Francesco Martucci
Viale Giulio Douhet, 11, 81100 Caserta CE, Italy

I Tigli
Via Camporosolo, 11, 37047 San Bonifacio VR
Italy

Joe & Pats
Joe Pappalardo
1758 Victory Boulevard, Staten Island, NY
USA

L'Antica Pizzeria Da Michele
Michele Condurro
Via Cesare Sersale, 1/3 80139
Napoli, Italy

L&B Spumoni Gardens
Ludovico Barbati
2725 86th St, Brooklyn, NY 11223
USA

La Pratolina
Via degli Scipioni, 248, 00192
Rome, Italy

Lee's Tavern
Kevin Hennessy and Eddie Canlon
60 Hancock St, Staten Island, NY 10305
USA

Li Rioni
Via dei Santissimi Quattro, 24, 00184,
Rome, Italy

Lombardi's
32 Spring St, New York, NY 10012, USA

Modern Apizza
Bill Pustari
874 State St, New Haven, CT 06511, USA

Neighbourhood
Istedgade 27, 1650 København
Denmark

Papa's Tomato Pies
Joe Papa
19 Robbinsville Allentown Rd, Robbinsville, NJ 08691
USA

Parziales
Angelo Parziale
80 Prince Street in Boston's North End
Boston, MA 02113, USA

Pepe In Grani
Franco Pepe
Vicolo S. Giovanni Battista, 3 81013 Caiazzo CE
Italy

Pequod's
Keith Jackson
2207 N Clybourn Ave, Chicago, IL 60614, USA

Pizano's Pizza & Pasta
Rudy Malnati Sr.
864 N State St, Chicago, IL 60610, USA

Studio Tamaki
東麻布 1-24-6-105 (4,146.49 mi)
Minato-ku, Tokyo, Japan 1060044

Pizzarias

Pizzarium
Gabriele Bonci
Via della Meloria, 43, 00136
Rome, Italy

Pizzeria Bianco
Chris Bianco
623 E Adams St Phoenix, AZ 85004, USA

Pizzeria Brandi
Raffaele Esposito
Salita S. Anna di Palazzo, 1/2, 80132
Napoli, Italy

Pizzeria Due
Ike Sewell
619 N Wabash Ave (8,540.23 mi)
Chicago, Illinois 60611, USA

Pizzería La Mezzetta
Abelardo, Gervasio and Marcelino
Av Alvarez Thomas 1321, Buenos Aires,
Argentina

Pizzeria UNO
Ike Sewell
29 E Ohio Street, North Side Chicago, IL, USA

Razza Pizza Artiginale
Dan Richer
275 Grove St, Jersey City, NJ 07302, USA

Santarpio's
Santarpio family
111 Chelsea St Boston, MA 02128, USA

Savoy
Motoazabu, Minato,
Tokyo, Japan

Seirinkan
2 Chome-6-4 Kamimeguro, Meguro
Tokyo 153-0051, Japan

Sforno
Stefano Callegari
Via Statilio Ottato, 110, 00175
Roma, Italy

Spago
Eddie Leung
176 N Canon Dr Beverly Hills, CA 90210,
USA

Story Deli
Ann Shore and Lee Hollingworth
The Shoulder of Mutton, 30 Church Street
Little Horwood Buckinghamshire MK17 0PF

Tommaso's
The Crotti and Cantalupo families
1042 Kearny St, San Francisco, CA 94133, USA

Umberto's
Umberto Corteo
633 Jericho Turnpike, New Hyde Park, NY 11040, USA

Zuppardi's Apizza
Anthony Zuppardi
179 Union Ave, West Haven, CT 06516, USA